D1524484

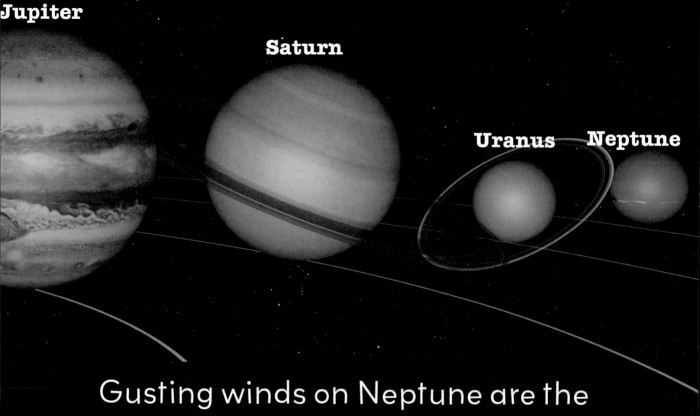

Jupiter

Saturn

Uranus   Neptune

Gusting winds on Neptune are the strongest in our solar system. Its winds are ten times more powerful than our strongest hurricanes on Earth.

Planet Watching

The more we study the gas planets, the more we are able to learn about our fascinating neighbors in space.

There is an amazing universe to discover just above your head!

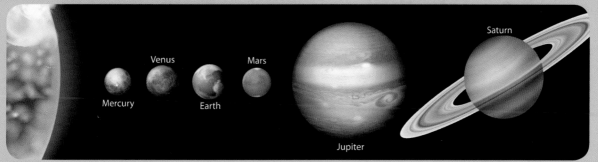

Mercury

Venus

Earth

Mars

Jupiter

Saturn

Five planets can be seen from Earth without any special tools: Mercury, Venus, Mars, Jupiter, and Saturn. A sky chart can show you where to look.

The planets look like small points of light in the sky, but they don't twinkle like stars do. Stars twinkle because they make their own light, while planets reflect light from the Sun.

Photo Glossary

atmosphere (AT-muhss-fihr): Mixture of gasses that surround a planet.

gravity (GRAV-uh-tee): The force that presses down on objects, keeping them from floating into space.

orbits (OR-bits): The paths objects follow around a star or planet.

 **planet** (PLAN-it): A round body in space that orbits the Sun.

 **rotates** (ROH-tates): To spin around on an axis, or center.

 **solar system** (SOH-lur SISS-tuhm): The Sun and all the objects that orbit around it, including Earth.

Index

Websites

www.amazing-space.stsci.edu/
www.nasa.gov/audience/forkids/kidsclub
   /flash/index.html#.UqSyyeLOR7x
www.starchild.gsfc.nasa.gov/docs/
   StarChild/StarChild.html

Meet The Author!
www.meetREMauthors.com

About the Author

Kyla Steinkraus lives with her husband and two children in Tampa, Florida. She enjoys drawing, photography, and writing. On hot summer nights, her family likes to lie down in the grass and gaze up at the sky.

www.rourkeeducationalmedia.com

PHOTO CREDITS: Cover and title page © Orla; page 4-5 © Procy, page 5 © Vectomart; page 6-7 © Andrea Danti; page 8 © Tristan3D, page 9 © Andrea Danti; page 10 courtesy NASA, page 11 © Tristan3D; page 12 © MarcelClemens, page 13 courtesy NASA; page 15 © Milagli; page 17 © MarcelClemens; page 18-19 © Naeblys; page 20 © Pete Pahham, page 21 inset © BlueRingMedia, page 21 © Nevada31; page 22 top to bottom © Pete Pahham, Asier Romero, dalmingo; page 23 top to bottom © MarcelClemens, LSkywalker, Vadim Sadovski

Edited by: Jill Sherman

Cover design and Interior design by: Nicola Stratford nicolastratford.com

Library of Congress PCN Data

Giant Gas Planets / Kyla Steinkraus
(Inside Outer Space)
ISBN 978-1-62717-728-3 (hard cover)
ISBN 978-1-62717-850-1 (soft cover)
ISBN 978-1-62717-962-1 (e-Book)
Library of Congress Control Number: 2014935654

Rourke Educational Media
Printed in the United States of America, North Mankato, Minnesota

Also Available as:
ROURKE'S e-Books

INSIDE OUTER SPACE

GIANT Gas Planets

Kyla Steinkraus

Rourke
Educational Media

rourkeeducationalmedia.com

Teaching Focus:

Word Study: Count the syllables in the words atmosphere and gravity. Which word has more syllables?
Which word has more letters?

Before Reading:

Building Academic Vocabulary and Background Knowledge

Before reading a book, it is important to set the stage for your child or student by using pre-reading strategies. This will help them develop their vocabulary, increase their reading comprehension, and make connections across the curriculum.

1. Read the title and look at the cover. *Let's make predictions about what this book will be about.*
2. Take a picture walk by talking about the pictures/photographs in the book. Implant the vocabulary as you take the picture walk. Be sure to talk about the text features such as headings, Table of Contents, glossary, bolded words, captions, charts/diagrams, or Index.
3. Have students read the first page of text with you then have students read the remaining text.
4. Strategy Talk – use to assist students while reading.
  - Get your mouth ready
  - Look at the picture
  - Think…does it make sense
  - Think…does it look right
  - Think…does it sound right
  - Chunk it – by looking for a part you know
5. Read it again.
6. After reading the book complete the activities below.

Content Area Vocabulary
Use glossary words in a sentence.

atmosphere
gravity
orbits
planet
rotates
solar system

After Reading:

Comprehension and Extension Activity

After reading the book, work on the following questions with your child or students in order to check their level of reading comprehension and content mastery.

1. *Name the four gas planets.* (Summarize)
2. *If the gas planets are made up of liquid and gas, how can they keep their round shape?* (Asking questions)
3. *Which planet has 63 moons and is the largest planet in the solar system?* (Summarize)
4. *Which two planets are sister planets?* (Summarize)

Extension Activity

There are four gas planets in our solar system. Choose one of the planets and create a trading card for it. Be sure to include basic information such as size, color, and climate. On the back of the card add interesting facts about the planet you chose. Share your card with your classmates.

Table of Contents

Gas Giants

What are all those lights twinkling above us at night? Most are stars, but a few of them are planets.

A **planet** is a round body in space that **orbits**, or circles, the Sun. A planet also **rotates**, or spins, on its axis. An axis is an imaginary line through the center of the planet.

Nearly all of the planets rotate in a counterclockwise direction.

Uranus

Neptune

Mars

Venus

Jupiter

SUN

Mercury

Earth

Saturn

There are eight planets in our **solar system.** The four planets farthest from the Sun are the gas giants. They are Jupiter, Saturn, Uranus, and Neptune.

Sun

Jupiter

Gas planets have many moons as well as rings that circle around them. Some planets, especially Saturn, have very noticeable rings.

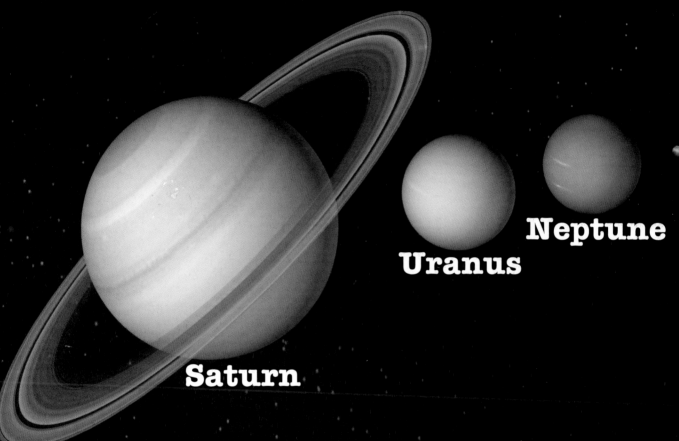

Saturn

Uranus

Neptune

These planets are not actually solid, but are made up of liquid and clouds of swirling gas. **Gravity** pulls the gas and liquid into a planet shape.

Giant Jupiter

Jupiter is the biggest planet in our solar system. It is so big that all the other planets could fit inside it.

Jupiter is orbited by at least 67 moons, more than any other planet.

Jupiter is a superhero! Jupiter helps Earth by protecting it from space objects that would hit it. Because of its large size and strong gravitational pull, comets and asteroids are pulled toward Jupiter and away from Earth. Thousands of space objects strike Jupiter every year.

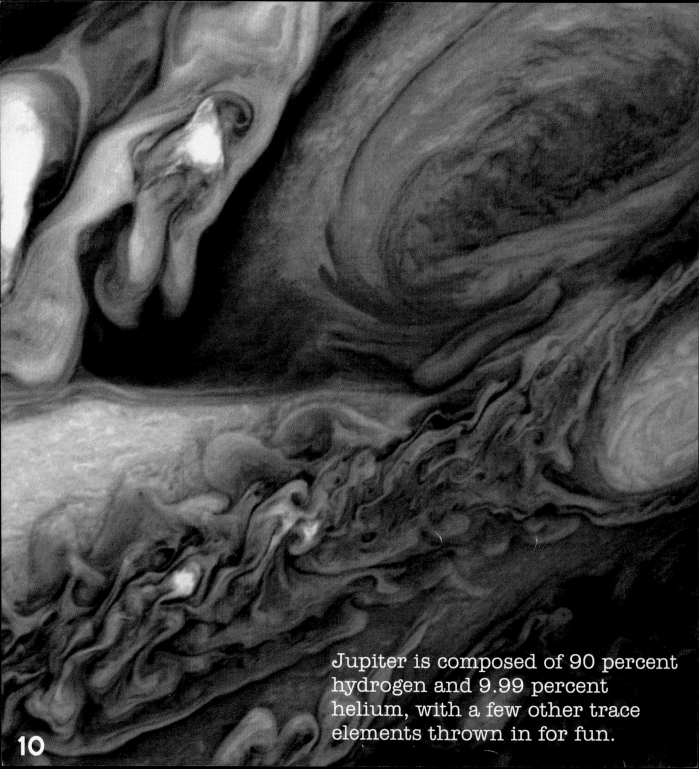

Jupiter is composed of 90 percent hydrogen and 9.99 percent helium, with a few other trace elements thrown in for fun.

It would be difficult to walk on Jupiter, since it has no solid surface at all! It is mostly made of gusting, swirling gasses that create massive, hurricane-like storms.

The Great
Red Spot

One of Jupiter's storms is so large that it can be seen from Earth. The Great Red Spot is a storm that began more than 300 years ago.

The Ringed Planet

Saturn is made mostly of light hydrogen gas. If you could find a bathtub big enough to hold it, Saturn would float!

Saturn is surrounded by seven thin rings made of sparkling chunks of dust-covered ice and rock.

Some of the ice chunks that form Saturn's rings are as tiny as dust particles. Some are as big as houses.

Topsy Turvy Uranus

Uranus is tipped on its side. It rotates sideways, like a giant Ferris wheel. Its many rings and moons circle from top to bottom.

Because Uranus moves slowly and has a long way to travel, it takes 84 Earth years for Uranus to travel one time around the Sun.

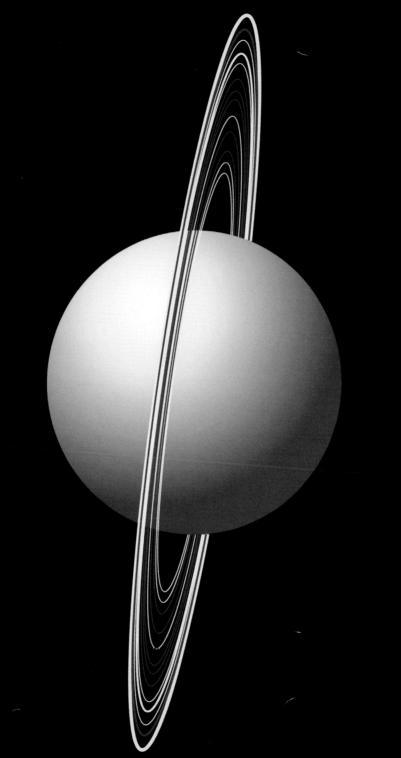

Uranus is mostly made of a slushy mixture of half-frozen water, ammonia, and methane. The methane gas scatters blue light, making Uranus appear blue.

It may be raining diamonds right now on the gas planets. The carbon soot created in the stormy atmosphere turns to diamonds under the intense pressure of each planet's atmosphere.

Uranus and its sister planet, Neptune, are very similar. Neptune also appears very blue because of the methane gas in its **atmosphere.**

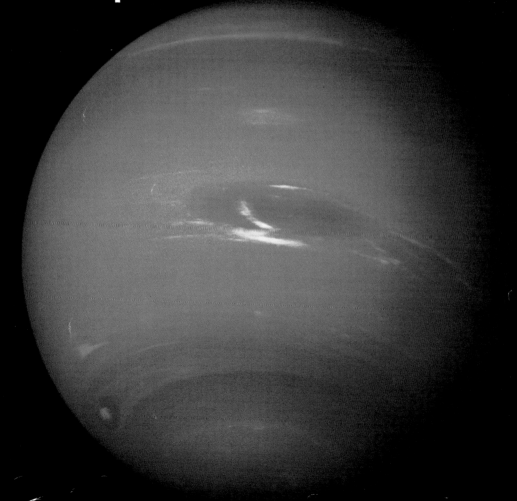

Ice Planet

Because Neptune is farthest from the Sun, it is the coldest planet.

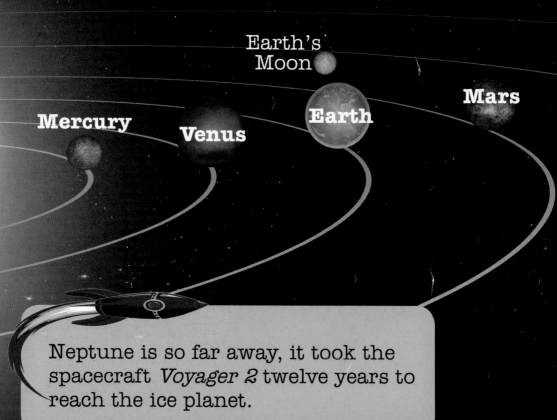

Earth's Moon

Mercury

Venus

Earth

Mars

Neptune is so far away, it took the spacecraft *Voyager 2* twelve years to reach the ice planet.